How The Bible Is An Irish Book

Altered And Adapted By

British-Roman Transcribers

Conor MacDari

Kessinger Publishing's Rare Reprints

Thousands of Scarce and Hard-to-Find Books on These and other Subjects!

- Americana
- Ancient Mysteries
- Animals
- Anthropology
- Architecture
- Arts
- Astrology
- Bibliographies
- Biographies & Memoirs
- Body, Mind & Spirit
- Business & Investing
- Children & Young Adult
- Collectibles
- Comparative Religions
- Crafts & Hobbies
- Earth Sciences
- Education
- Ephemera
- Fiction
- Folklore
- Geography
- Health & Diet
- History
- Hobbies & Leisure
- Humor
- Illustrated Books
- Language & Culture
- Law
- Life Sciences
- Literature
- Medicine & Pharmacy
- Metaphysical
- Music
- Mystery & Crime
- Mythology
- Natural History
- Outdoor & Nature
- Philosophy
- Poetry
- Political Science
- Science
- Psychiatry & Psychology
- Reference
- Religion & Spiritualism
- Rhetoric
- Sacred Books
- Science Fiction
- Science & Technology
- Self-Help
- Social Sciences
- Symbolism
- Theatre & Drama
- Theology
- Travel & Explorations
- War & Military
- Women
- Yoga
- *Plus Much More!*

**We kindly invite you to view our catalog list at:
http://www.kessinger.net**

CHAPTER V

THE BIBLE AN IRISH BOOK ALTERED AND ADAPTED BY BRITISH-ROMAN TRANSCRIBERS

ALTHOUGH our Christian peoples, in the more advanced countries of today, have denounced Jewish pogroms and deliberately planned murders of Jewish people in some of the countries of eastern Europe during the World War, what can they think of the wholesale deportations and murders and suffering inflicted upon the people of what is now called Syria when they know that the Roman Church put her plan in operation to charge them with having crucified the ideal Savior Jesu (The Sun God) and scattered them broadcast over the world. By dispersing those people, she cleared the way for the renaming of places in Judea to make it appear that such a man as Jesus had lived there; that those various places said to have been the scenes of his life and travels were actually real places and in existence on the map with those names. It is something awful to contemplate, but the Roman Church did this thing; and the people whom she punished thus and who bear the undeserved stigma to this day for crucifying the Savior are as innocent of such a deed as the child unborn.

The Roman fathers employed most ingenious methods to establish the "authenticity" of Jesus. To that end they had stories written up purporting to be by certain men, some of whom denied his God-like powers, while there were other witnesses who declared that he worked wonders. Her scribes also wrote up accounts of those who were supposed to be his companions, but written in such a way that their stories would not agree in every minute detail but near enough so that it would not appear that one account was a copy of the other. It must be as a witness giving a different and distinctly individual narration of the facts as seen by himself.

These trained fabricators considered that no two or more persons would write the facts regarding an event in real life in just the same identical words, so it was thought best to have a little variation inserted in the accounts as given by "Matthew, Mark, Luke, and John." So that is how we find it arranged in those four books by the Roman doctors. If Luke tells of an event in one way, John tells it a little differently, and so with Matthew and Mark. Luke records that the miraculous draught of fishes was made at the beginning of the ministry of Jesus (V: 6). John says that it did not happen until after he had risen from the dead (John XXI: 11). John says that, although the number of fish was great, the net was not broken; and Luke says that their net did break (V: 6).

Matthew says that Jesus told the twelve apostles to go and preach, and commanded them to "provide neither gold nor silver, nor brass in your purses, nor scrip for your journey, neither two coats, neither shoes, nor yet staves" (Matt. X: 9, 10). Mark is made to mention the same incident just a little bit different and with a slight contradiction of his "infallible" brother scribe. He says that Jesus commanded them to take nothing for their journey save a staff only (Mark V: 1–8).

Like inconsistencies which are so many in these four gospels stamp them as counterfeit books. In fact, the very names of the authors to whom these books are ascribed are forgeries and misleading. They were intended so to be; for it was claimed that they were "Hebrew," while the plain truth is that they were taken entire from the ideals of the Irish Gospels with the nomenclature slightly changed in order to escape detection.

It is not my purpose to give an extensive elucidation or explanation of the Bible in this chapter or work, but as the Irish Bible and Irish Great Pyramid of Iesa are closely related in spiritual and symbolic significance as agencies and landmarks for the guidance of "wayfaring" mankind in its progress upward toward spiritual enlightenment and regeneration, for this reason I feel I must touch upon this phase in my theme specifically, if only briefly. As I have shown by citations that forgeries were committed, I shall prove by explanations that our Bible is an Irish book, of pre-Roman times, and an out-and-out theft without acknowledgment from the Irish Church of Iesa. Any competent person who knows the Irish language cannot fail to recognize it.

Our present version of the Bible then is an authorized adaptation from the original Irish scriptures with alterations and additions made from time to time by

Roman and British churchmen in secrecy as they deemed it necessary and advisable to do so.

The following agreement in the writings under the names of "Matthew," "Mark" and "Luke," regarding the impression made upon the people by the teachings of Jesus, is an example which shows plainly the work of the forging priests. It would be impossible for such agreement to have occurred in the original writings of any three men writing individually and independently on any subject whatsoever, but in fabrication from the older works and collaborating, the priest-scribes simply blundered and made each of the three "witnesses" write down and repeat the same identical expression in "copy" as to how Jesus impressed the people.

Here is the forged testimony:

Matthew says: "They were astonished at his doctrine" (XXII : 33).

Mark says: "They were astonished at his doctrine" (I : 22).

Luke says: "They were astonished at his doctrine" (LV : 32).

Many authors and critics have commented upon and pointed out the inaccuracies and inconsistencies of the scriptures and many of them have stated their firm belief that they were copied from older books. But none of them could obtain a clue beyond a surmise which was far from the truth and none of them was able to produce the real facts which were necessary to convince. But the work that they did has helped and made it possible to accomplish the desired end. They found so many flaws in it, which the "jugglers" did not cover up, that it kept the question open until the solution was found. The true source has escaped discovery until now; at least it has never before been disclosed to the knowledge of mankind as a whole.

The Irish Scriptures were altered and adapted to the scheme of the church in order to make the fable of Iesa an historical and geographical fact. Names from the Scriptures were given to places in Syria during its occupation by the Crusaders to bear this out. It also suited the purpose of British statecraft to obscure and suppress all evidence of the greatness and culture of the Irish Nation, than whom no people in the world's history have reached greater heights both spiritually and intellectually nor have suffered greater injustice at the hands of priestly imposters or political oppressors.

The men who were engaged in executing this literary fraud committed as well the audacious crime of completely effacing all evidence of credit due the Irish Nation for the most brilliant and glorious service to civilization and human enlightenment. It almost passes belief that a fraud so stupendous could escape so long without discovery. But when we consider the thoroughness and extent to which the plot was carried out, and the magnitude of the forces which were employed in the work, it is not so much to be wondered at, forces such as the Roman Empire, with its world power, then the Roman Catholic Church and the British Kingdom, with propaganda systematically spread abroad in order to create a false impression of everything pertaining to the past history of Ireland and her people. These are the forces which have perpetrated and profited by this great fraud. The deception is still continued and the secret jealously guarded by both the Roman Church and Britain from the world at large, but more particularly from the Irish people who have suffered so much from those two adverse forces. The men who executed this plot were acting jointly in the interest of both Rome and Britain. Even to this day, the British Government does not encourage, even if it will allow, excavations or investigations to be made about the hill of Tara in Ireland (Rev. Joseph Wild in *When the World Comes to an End*).

I will give two citations here, with more to follow, to show that the names of many of the characters in the Bible are plainly Irish, and it is because of this fact that the Irish Roman Catholic priests would not allow the Irish Catholics to read the Bible. They were told not to read it, that "it was not a sufficient rule of faith." The real reason was that some of the Irish people might recognize the Irish names in a "Jewish" Bible and ask questions that it would embarrass them to answer satisfactorily. Nevertheless, it is a very astonishing thing that what now appears so clearly fraudulent could have escaped detection for so long a time. There are three main reasons for this: first, that the people are slow to attribute fraud and dishonesty to the clergy; second, that the Irish Catholics who could speak the Irish language believed, as they were told by the priests, that the Bible was brought to them from outside instead of being of Irish origin, and, being uninstructed in the principles of man's nature, were not given to investigation or research for spiritual truth; and third, that the field of religious literature has been dominated by the works of professional preachers and other religionists who have kept up the delusion knowingly or who took it for granted that the published accounts of the origin of the Scriptures were, in the main, true and were originally written in Greek with one single copy in Hebrew, as has always been asserted. It will, therefore, be a surprise to Bible readers of today who have had no suspicion of this deception to be told that it was through the medium of the Irish language that the true key would be found for the solution of the mystery of the origin of the Bible. The proof of this fact is here given for all mankind to see and know.

The first of the two citations to be given in this chapter is from the Book of John (Ch. 3, 23d verse). "And John was baptizing in Aenon near to Salem, because there was much water there; and they came and were baptized."

In the latest revision of the Bible, the "Doctors" have altered the word Aenon and have made it Enon. In the older version it is Aenon. This is a compound of two Irish words, Aen, meaning a circle of the Sun, a year, and On, also a name of the Sun. The complete word itself means the Sun. The word On also signifies cause, reason, swiftness, fierceness, eagerness, excellent, noble, good, also wolfdog. These are qualities and attributes associated with and applied to the Solar Sun and to the Sun God by the Aryan or Irish Priests of Iesa. Their theology was based on the idea that the Supreme Deity never had nor has a name. He is known only by attributes, as the "Good" or God, Holy, Most High, etc. And, as the Solar Sun is the center of light and His great representative or "Son" in our system, the Sun God is named after the qualities and attributes of some idea, such as "the Horseman"or "Charioteer," "the Strong One," or "Samson," or "the Fierce One," Horus, "the Heavenly Wolf Who is Eager," swift and fierce.

The Irish, during their sojourn in Egypt, gave the name of On to one of their cities on the Nile. The City of On, the City of the Sun, was afterwards called Heliopolis by the Greeks and Romans. Salem is a "Hebrew" word, but the basis of it is in the Irish word Solas, light. As "Hebrew" is a jargon of the Irish, it follows more or less closely the root it is taken from, as will be seen. So Salem means the City of God or Light.

The meaning of this myth is that John (Aen — the Sun) was baptizing in Aenon, the City of the Sun, near to Salem, the City of God, in the realm of Light, the celestial kingdom. Where else could such a being as the pure and perfected man be said to dwell? In this myth, John, (Aen, Eion, or Ain, three forms of the word and all pronounced Ain) represents the redeemed and glorified man, man at the highest stage of spiritual attainment, next to the Messianic state, so that in his next succeeding life or incarnation here again on earth

he will be the Messiah.   In the Irish mythic narrative
of the Bible we see that, after John, the prophet and
holy man, comes the perfected Man-God, the Messiah,
Iesa (Jesus).

This is an example of the esoteric truth and wisdom
which lies hidden beneath the veil of the scriptural
allegory as formulated by those inspired Irish Adepts,
and though they have been denied the credit of author-
ship through a thieves' compact of silence, their wisdom
and their works still exist in both the Bible and The
Great Pyramid of Iesa.

The second citation to prove that the Bible is Irish,
purely and unmistakably so (and I defy contradiction),
is taken from the Books of Mark and Samuel.

The Pharisees questioned Jesus because the disciples
plucked ears of corn on the Sabbath.   He said: "Have
ye never read what David did when he had need . . . ?
How he went into the house of God in the days of Abiathar the High Priest, and did eat the shrewbread, which
is not lawful to eat but for the priests?" (Mark II:
24, 25, 26.)

The first Book of Samuel contains this version of
David and the shewbread: "Then came David to Nob
to Ahimelech the priest. . . .   So the priest gave him
hallowed bread; for there was no other bread there but
the shewbread, that was taken from before the Lord."
(Chap. 21, 1–6.)

The foregoing is but a cryptic allusion to the perfect-
ing work of the Initiate who is engaged in the effort of
eradicating from his nature all worldly ambitions and

the desires of the flesh for the development of his higher self, the Solar Body, the God within himself.

The word Abiathar, the name of the High Priest, is such a plain and easily recognized Irish word that even the uneducated Irishman or Scotsman, who is able to speak Gaelic, can understand it, and will recognize it at once as a word of Irish or Gaelic speech. It is a compound of two words. The word "Ab" means lord or father, and "Athar" is also the word for "father." The two words combined would literally be "father-father." The literal sense of it would be "Head-Father," for the word Ab is applied to the head of a monastery; but the esoteric sense of it is High Father or God. The vowel letter *i* is introduced to connect the two words into one. The Roman-British scribe in this instance gives us a compound Irish word, and, of course, without the least suggestion that such is the case, makes a play on the name and presents it to us in the English version of the Bible as the name of the "Hebrew" high priest.

It is a priestly deception, as will be seen readily, on the part of the transcriber of Mark, when we understand that the character "David" and the incident connected with him is but a story invented for the purpose of containing an idea, as follows: Abiathar in this allegory alludes to the "High Father God," manifesting spiritually through the Solar-Sun, in his human counterpart, which is the Solar or luminous spiritual body of the initiate "David," who is on the upward path, striving for the victory of the spirit over matter, in the material body or flesh. This should be instructive to every wayfaring man who is traveling Eastward towards the dawn from darkness to light into whose hands these pages may come, as well as to the general body of Bible readers.

The copyist and transcriber who has given us the version ascribed to "Samuel" has "David" go to Nob to Ahimelech the priest. The word Nob is Irish and is spelled Noeb, but it is pronounced as if it were Na-ev, with the *o* having a short sound as *oe*. If the word was written by the priests without the intent to deceive, they would have presented it to us in this form — Nob, the dot over the *b* making it *v* or *bh*, which, in the Irish, has the sound of *v*. They have taken advantage of the alphabetical features of the Irish language to perpetrate a fraud on the people of the world. The word Nob means Heaven, sacred or holy. The word Ahimelech means the Heavenly King or Solar-Sun, who is figuratively a champion, hero, or ruler. Melchezedech is another form of the word from the same root. The letter *a* is pronounced broad, as if it were *aw*. The letter *h* is added to it for an aspirate to soften it. Together they form a prefix. "Melech" is the "Hebraized" or jargonized form of the Irish word Miol, an animal or ideal for the Sun. As the Sun moves swiftly, it is in imagination Miol, an animal. It is the figurative name given to the Sun by the Irish priests of Iesa. Therefore, the Sun is called Miolchu, pronounced Melchu, a greyhound. It is also called Onchu, a wolf. Hence, the terms applied to the Sun, "The Swift One,"

"The Fierce One." The greyhound and the wolf-hound have ever been favorites with the Irish and figure in their legends and fables. We see the same deception practiced by the Irish Roman priesthood upon the Irish Catholics of our own day in the word Melcho, a name of the Personified Sun. He is the fictitious person to whom, in the story, "St. Patrick" was sold as a slave. Thus proving to us again that the lying and dishonest priests of Rome wrote a false and worthless history for the Irish people.

They are the people who stole the ancient Irish Bible and palmed it off on the world as a "Jewish" book, produced by a people over in Syria. It is an invention and an imposture on the world.

The Irish word for wolfdog is On. Hence, the Irish priests of Iesa, during the sojourn of the Irish race in Egypt, gave the name to a city on the Nile. They also applied the name Onchu, the wolf, to the Sun; therefore, we have the "Heavenly Wolf" Osiris, meaning the "High Eastern Sun" (from Os, high, and Soir, pronounced Sir and meaning East, — hence the Morning Sun). He is Horus, "The Risen," from the Irish word Or, aspirated to Hor, meaning a Lord or Savior, one to whom prayer is offered. The word also means "From Whom," in the sense of descent. Hence we find the Horus is the son of Osiris.

In the mythical idea, the Sun is Osiris in the early morning and he becomes Horus, the Risen Sun and Savior, in the early forenoon. He is the wolf Horus at noon when his rays are hot and oppressive, also Typhon, the Evil One. He is the Lord and Savior given to the Egyptian people to worship by the Irish priests of Iesa. Here are the facts that defy contradiction; the Irish language is the treasure house in which these indisputable proofs exist for everyone who wishes to view them. With the truths disclosed in these pages mankind is confronted with a new and altered viewpoint which gives us a new conception of history. The priest and churchman has imposed upon the credulity of the professor. A new perspective opens before us, and scholars and honest minded men and women must address themselves to the task of straightening out the confused and unreliable accounts of the past which have emanated from such obviously self-interested sources as Rome and Britain.

Ahimelech, then, like Abiathar, is God, in his aspect of the Solar King or Sun, whose Divine Human Aspect is the perfected man. Therefore, in this myth, we are told that David ate the shewbread, that is, he received the sacred wisdom of the priests, practiced abstemiousness and self-denial and came into a state of holiness from which he advances to the perfect or Messianic state. And so, from the advancing David, the Messiah is born. Hence, Jesus is said to be born of the "House of David." Thus it is to the Irish Magian Adepts of the ancient religion of Iesa that we are indebted for the knowledge of these esoteric spiritual truths, preserved under the veil of allegory and myth.

The distinction and renown which the Magi gave to Ireland, which island in mythology is referred to as the

"Isle of the Blest," has been taken to herself by Rome, as if it all had come about since her ministration there; hence, the allusion made by her priests to Ireland as the "Island of Saints," that is, Roman Saints. Those great men developed the powers of the soul and became God-like, while their Roman successors have become renowned for their capacity for acquiring stocks and bonds and become distinguished according to their ability as investors.

They have denied to the ancient Irish Masters of Wisdom all acknowledgment of their indebtedness and blotted out so far as they could the very memory of their existence, ascribing their erudition and wisdom to others and they mention them only to traduce them. They covertly refer to them as the "snakes" which "St. Patrick" banished from the island, while the multitude is taught to believe that it was the creeping reptiles of the dust that he banished. The latter never did exist in Ireland (*The Esoteric Club*, by Rev. Canon Lynch of Cork, Ireland). They do not apply to them the dignified term of "serpent," which is the symbol of wisdom, but "snakes" to imply what is low and evil. Baseness could go no further.

The Irish race has suffered humiliation even to this day, through this willful traduction and carefully directed perversion of their history. Fables have been invented and taught to the people as genuine facts and bona-fide history. The writer has, like others, absorbed a lot of their fiction and must confess it was some task to unlearn it and to adjust his mind to the reception of even obvious truths, which conflicted with pious "untruths." It is certainly a preposterous thing to allow a body of pretentious impostors to instill their falsehoods into the minds of the growing youth. Moreover, this political priesthood insults our intelligence by considering themselves solely as "God's anointed" and His special favorites. We are told that in England and Ireland it was the practice to give the priests in many places a number of shares of distillery stock as provision for their "future." The priests speak of their churches as "plants," just as if they were factories, and they are fitted up with slot receptacles to catch any fractional currency which might either by advice or suggestion be enticed from the pockets of the worshipers.

It is safe to say that light is advancing and that truth is progressing regardless of this reactionary force, which is now exposed for the first time in a manner which reveals their plot. It cannot help but open the eyes of mankind to the great fraud, and more especially awaken the Irish people who have been so foully betrayed and sold into the hands of their oppressors.

In the citations which I have given to show and prove that the Bible is an Irish Book, the names of places and the names of characters given show plainly the direct connection with and their derivation from the Irish. The elucidation of "The Great Pyramid" and of the topic "Egypt" will add to this proof, so that anyone who comes with open mind and unbiased judgment will not fail to see it. Every lover of truth, qualified to judge, will be convinced that the names are Irish and only slightly changed in the form and spelling, changed only enough to deceive the unsuspecting. It is seldom that a man arises outside the ranks of the clergy who develops a knowledge of the elements upon which the religious myth is constructed. To solve the mystery of the origin of the Bible, this knowledge and that of the Irish language, combined with a true perspective of history, was necessary. It required also a true insight into Ireland's past and the villainous intrigues of the Roman and British priesthoods and the rôle they played in shaping events of momentous consequence in world affairs. To conceal those facts from posterity, they had recourse to the scheme of falsifying the world's history and substituting therefore a tissue of lies and inventions.

The British propaganda has been fostered by the government Board of Education and such misleading works as Pennock's "Catechism of the History of Ireland" which were put into the Irish school system. Persecution and propaganda have served the purpose intended and have caused the Catholic Irish to place an almost blind belief in the integrity of their priests who are a part of the Roman Church and ably doing the work of Rome in carrying on this deception, while the English churchman has done his part to the same end, namely, to keep knowledge of Ireland's great past history under cover of oblivion.

The Irish Catholics were directed away from a study of the Bible instead of towards it and made to depend on what the priests saw fit to dole out to them. Otherwise it is reasonable to suppose that long before this day, some Irish-speaking person could not have failed to detect the idiomatic Irish in the very warp and woof of the Old Testament. It is an undeniable fact that the Irish-speaking Roman Catholics were not frequent readers, much less students, of the Bible. I have laid some stress on this phase of my theme, but not inordinately so, considering that I am announcing the greatest discovery in the history of all literature, that the Bible is Irish and of Irish origin. I am aware that this will be a shock and surprise to students and intellectuals in all the enlightened countries of the world, to be shown that they have been made the victims of a fraud. It was bound to be discovered in time, for truth so evident could not be hidden forever from the minds that were free from bias. Anyone qualified to approach the truth could not fail to see it, even though the schemers were reiterating their claims through the press and from all the pulpits in Christendom.

There is no doubt in the writer's mind but that the inner circles in British Statecraft and High Church, as well as those of the Roman Church in Britain and Ireland, are keenly aware of this truth and carefully guard the secret of their fraud. A few years ago, the writer read a History of Ireland by Thomas Moore, the famous poet and author, in which he bewailed the fact that at every turn in his quest for knowledge and facts he found a conspiracy of silence and suppression. He produced his work under just such discouraging conditions, but he rendered a service to posterity by publishing his observations of the attitude of those persons who were in a position to assist him in his search for facts, had they wished to do so.

My studies and investigations have enabled me to discover facts and truths as presented here and these truths will stand every investigation. It all goes to prove that even the cleverest forgers and falsifiers are not safe from exposure and discovery. So it is the case with the Roman and British forgers. Although the imposition of the Savior Jesus, and the substitution of him for Iesa, brought great riches to the Roman Church, it required a great and tremendous effort to succeed in making it appear to the world that he had an actual historical existence.

The people were in a terrible state of ignorance and superstition, a condition which was favorable to the Church in effecting this cherished idea. Her ambition to make that one project alone successful was the cause of inflicting untold misery and suffering upon the people of three continents during the wars of the Crusades, which were instituted for that end. The Roman Church was obliged to enlist practically all Europe in these wars. It is estimated that there were two million lives lost in carrying out that scheme in the struggle to drive the Mohammedans out of Syria in the tenth and eleventh centuries. It was during the occupancy of the so-called Holy Land by the Crusaders for a period of 87 years that Rome gave the names to the localities and places there which are mentioned in the Scriptures, and which names had not been before identified with such places.

During that time they did everything that they thought necessary or that circumstances would permit in preparing the ground to place marks of identification about each locality which was selected to be the birth-place or scene of activity of each of the mythical char-acters to whose fictitious existence special significance or prominence was to be given.

Such, for instance, is the example of the patriarchal character "Abraham" whom they assigned to the "Land of Ur" in Chaldea. Ur is an idiomatic Irish word, and means the Sun, fire, and the East. The word also ex-presses an Irish idea or conception of Heaven. Ur is connected with the fabulous Irish land Tir-na-N'og — the land of the young, or the land of perpetual youth. The meaning of Ur in this instance is fresh, green, plenty, new (not stale or old), liberal, the land of plen-tiousness, the Heavenly Kingdom. And Abraham him-self is most obviously an Irish idea of the personified Sun. There can be no room for doubt as to this fact as he comes from Ur (the Sun), and, to be true to Irish mythic form, each syllable of his name is a name of the Sun. The word Ab is an Irish name for father, and here signifies Father or Creator Sun. And Rah means the moving or revolving Sun. And Am means time, for the Sun is the Governor and Lord of Time and Regu-lator of the seasons. And, furthermore, as Abraham is the Sun, he comes from Ur in Chaldea. Chaldea is a mythical and fictitious name falsely said to be of a

country in Asia. The name is from the Irish word Caul
- (a veil, secret, hidden), meaning mystically the Great
Unseen. A Culdee was an Irish religious ascetic of the
worship of Iesa, a seer.

Abraham has two female consorts, one of whom he
marries. She is Sarah, from the Irish word Sor or Sorc
(Sark), meaning delight, light, pleasure, bright, con-
spicuous, clear, the day. The other woman was named
Hagar, from the root word Acor, meaning covetousness,
desire. She represents the night. The letter *h* is only
an auxiliary in the Irish alphabet and is used as an aspirate. But the "Doctors" have used it as a regular
letter for deceptive reasons in the formation of the name
of this mythic character. And, instead of using the
letter *c*, they use the *g*. These two letters, in the old
manuscripts, were often used one for the other indis-
criminately.

And so we have Hagar. And, as she is Desire, she is
not Abraham's true wife but his concubine. She bears
him a son, Ishmael (the Irish Ies-Moal). Ies is the
Sun, and Moal means bald. The young Sun, or early
morning Sun, is said to be bald as he has no rays until
later. So Ishmael is the young or morning Sun born
of the Night. So, in the Irish Bible myth, we find that
Abraham, the Sun, has two wives, Sarah the fair one,
the Day, and Hagar the dark one, the Night. Sarah
is jealous of Hagar the concubine and has Abraham
send her away. In the phenomena of Nature, the Day
always sends the Night away.

This is the end of this publication.

Any remaining blank pages are for our book binding requirements and are blank on purpose.

To search thousands of interesting publications like this one, please remember to visit our website at:

http://www.kessinger.net

Printed in the USA
CPSIA information can be obtained
at www.ICGtesting.com
LVHW081447050624
782384LV00006B/913

9 781162 847801